IN THE
ZONE

How To Live In The
Sweet Spot Of Success

by Ed Young

Published in Dallas, Texas, by EY Publishing.

All Scripture quotations, unless otherwise noted, are taken from The
Holy Bible, New International Version (North American Edition),
copyright © 1973, 1978, 1984 by the International Bible Society. Used
by permission of Zondervan Publishing House.

Scripture quotations marked (NLT) are taken from the Holy Bible, New
Living Translation, copyright © 1996. Used by permission of Tyndale
House Publishers, Inc., Wheaton, Illinois 60189. All rights reserved.

Scripture quotations marked (NKJV) are taken from the New King James
Version, copyright © 1979, 1980, 1982. Used by permission of Thomas
Nelson, Inc., Nashville, Tennessee. All rights reserved.

Scripture quotations marked (NASB) are taken from the New American
Standard Bible, copyright © The Lockman Foundation 1960, 1962,
1963, 1968, 1971, 1972, 1973, 1975, 1977. Used by permission.

Any emphases or parenthetical comments within Scripture are the
author's own.

Cover design and inside layout by Shane Dennehey.

ISBN 10: 0-9725813-8-3
ISBN 13: 978-0-9725813-8-7

What Pastors Around The Country Are Saying About *In The Zone*...

"I've been teaching the *'In the Zone'* message series at our church and God has really been blessing us with supernatural results. The last several weeks our budget giving is up approximately 40%!"

John Cross, Sr. Pastor
South Biscayne Baptist Church
North Port, FL

"I can't help but pass along exciting news about how God has used *'In the Zone'* to bring glory to Him through our local church...."

Ronnie Cordrey, Sr. Pastor
NorthStar Christian Church
Plainfield, IL

"While I was teaching *'In the Zone,'* people responded with amazing stories of how God is blessing them because of their decision to trust Him with their finances."

Kevin Webb, Sr. Pastor
Crossroads Christian Fellowship
San Bernardino, CA

"The material from *'In the Zone'* has had a huge influence on what we are attempting to do at our church. Thank you for your powerful teaching and straight forward message on such an important topic."

Paul Newell, Sr. Pastor
FamilyFellowship a Church for Family
Beaumont, CA

CONTENTS

DEDICATED TO THE PEOPLE OF FELLOWSHIP CHURCH...

Thank you for your faithful support these past sixteen years. Because of your willingness to sacrifice for others, Fellowship Church has become much more than a vision—it has become a reality. Your generosity continues to provide the perfect illustration of living in the zone. I am humbled by your dedication to the principles found in this book, and I look forward to walking with you as we continue to grow.

INTRODUCTION
Get Zoned In!

It happens in relationships—you surprise your spouse with the week-long cruise he or she has been dreaming of for years. It happens on the golf course—you birdie four straight holes on the back nine. It happens in the boardroom—you make a series of crucial decisions that significantly increases your company's bottom line.

It's during those moments that you feel it. And while you may not be able to articulate the feeling perfectly, you instinctively know that you are *"In the Zone."*

The greatest athletes in the world talk about the zone with awe and wonder. The major league pitcher one strike away from a no-hitter; the all-American quarterback who hasn't missed a pass the entire game; the point guard who drains three-pointer after three-pointer—they all experience the excitement and thrill of being in the zone.

But the zone isn't realized only by the professional athletes of the world or just in those moments when we experience an emotional high. There are much greater and further reaching implications to living in the zone.

We hear that phrase tossed around a lot these days—in the zone. But what exactly is the zone? Where is the zone? And what does it mean in your life and mine to live inside the zone?

Simply put, the zone is an area that is set apart, or is distinguished in some respect, from its adjoining areas. It's an area that stands in marked contrast to others around it.
In short, it's the sweet spot of life.

Certain times we are in relational zones. Other times we're in financial zones. Sometimes we're in athletic zones. But no matter what stage of life we find ourselves in, we would all like to live permanently in the zone; to have the thrills and chills of the zone overflow into every area of life. Just think how incredible it would be to live in a constant state of "zoneness"!

By reading this book and applying what you learn to your daily life, you can learn how to do just that. You will discover the path that God has strategically set out before you that leads to a full-time life in the zone.

One recurring, overpowering and undeniable truth will surface again and again as you discover the secrets to living in the zone. You are going to realize in the coming pages that our loving God is a God who is for you. He's not against you.

Too many people have an unexplainable and paralyzing fear that God is out to get them, that he doesn't want anything good to happen to them. But that could not be further from the truth. In spiritual terms, the zone is the sweet spot of God's success.

God has designed you and me with the intention that we spend our time on earth in the sweet spot of his success—not success in the world's terms, but God's definition of success in every area of life. He has custom designed each of us to be zoned in, not zoned out. Amazingly, though, most people have never heard or read in-dept﹨

Let me do a quick side﹍
that the enemy does not ﹍
not want you to get a h﹍
of that cold hard realit﹐﹍
this book is going to be diffic﹍
wild and wacky stuff will come into ﹐
face spiritual warfare, because Satan doesn﹐﹍
able to advance with the knowledge that you will ﹍
this book.

But don't give up. It's vitally important that you be in a mindset of prayer, humility and commitment as you dive into this material. Just simply pray, "God, open my life to your teaching. Deposit your truth into my account. I want to not only learn your truth, but also to apply what it means to live in the zone."

If you approach this topic with that mindset, God will equip you with the strength and determination to finish this book and, ultimately, to get zoned in!

CHAPTER ONE
GOD HEARTED

When my son EJ was about three years old, he wanted to be just like me, so he mimicked my every move. As I would get ready for my day each morning, EJ would follow me around like a shadow. I'd walk into the bathroom to brush my teeth and EJ would be right behind me, ready to brush his teeth. One morning as we were brushing our teeth, EJ was watching me spit into the sink. Wanting to mimic everything I did, EJ spit his toothpaste out—right onto the bathroom floor!

EJ wanted to put mousse in his hair when I did. He wanted to wear the same clothes I did. I remember one time he even poured himself a cup of coffee. He didn't actually drink it, but he thought it would be great to have a big mug of java in the morning just like Daddy.

He even copied the way I moved. One Saturday morning I was watching some basketball on television, and as I leaned back in my seat and crossed my legs, EJ did the same thing.

Essentially, the Bible tells us to do the exact same thing. Ephesians 5:1 says to "Be imitators of God." This word "imitator" in the Greek is where we get our English word "mimic" from. But it's not a once-a-lifetime thing, or a once-a-month thing, or a once-a-week thing. It is an every single second of every single day thing. We are called to continually mimic, imitate, our heavenly Father, as a child imitates his earthly father.

DISCOVERING GOD'S HEART

At the very outset, we must understand something that is critical to the rest of this book. **Living in the zone is first and foremost about seeing God as he really is and mimicking his character in our lives.** So many of us are zoned out because we do not understand who God is and what he is like—we don't understand his essence, his nature.

No one wants to be zoned out. We all want to be zoned in. And our heavenly Father desperately wants that for us as well. You may be thinking, "Well, okay. So God wants me to live in the zone. But what does that mean? What does that look like? How do I discover the secrets and experience the thrills and chills of the zone in my own life? Where do I start?"

To live in the zone we must first realize what is at the heart of God.

We see the very core of God's nature in perhaps the most well-known verse in the Bible: "For God so loved the world that he gave his one and only Son that whoever believes in him shall not perish but have eternal life" (John 3:16).

"For God so loved the world that he gave...." The essence

of God is generosity. That's what he is all about. People so often have a hard time accepting the fact that God is a God of generosity. But it's true. And because God is generous, he wants to give us good things. That's who he is.

As I mentioned earlier, the theme of this book is God is for us, not against us. That's the incredible promise found in Romans 8:31-32, "If God is for us, who can be against us? He who did not spare his own Son, but gave him up for us all—how will he not also, along with him, graciously give us all things?"

The truth is undeniable: God is generous and loves to give us good things. He is not a cosmic ogre. He does not delight in making us miserable. On the contrary, at the very heart of God is a perfectly generous and giving nature.

It's within the context of who God is that we need to, by faith, download a vital truth into our lives. I'll introduce it first and then unpack it as we go along. *God's generosity is evidenced through his blessings.*

That's a hard truth for us to accept in a what's-in-it-for-me, sin-soaked world. We don't trust anyone or anything. And to say that someone actually wants to give us good things, to bless us, just doesn't fit within our cynical point of view.

On one hand, we have a God who is a generous God. He is generous beyond anything our finite minds are able to comprehend. But on the other hand, Satan is saturated with selfishness, envy and pride. And because that real and evil presence is in the world, because sin entered the world, no one is a natural born giver.

We are all natural born takers. We enter this world with a

natural tendency to choose sin. And at the very heart of our sin nature is this saturation with selfishness, envy and pride.

That's why it is so difficult for us to comprehend God as a giver. We've become jaded by our own sinful, selfish nature and have a hard time accepting the love, grace, mercy of a generous God.

However, make no mistake about it, the Bible is clear and to the point that God wants to bless us. Consider the following:

Proverbs 10:22
The blessing of the Lord brings wealth, and he adds no trouble to it.

Psalm 29:11
The Lord gives strength to his people; the Lord blesses his people with peace.

Deuteronomy 28:2
All these blessings will come upon you and accompany you if you obey the Lord your God.

Psalm 112:1-3
Blessed is the man who fears the Lord,
who finds great delight in his commands.
His children will be mighty in the land;
the generation of the upright will be blessed.
Wealth and riches are in his house,
and his righteousness endures forever.

BLESS THIS AND BLESS THAT

We throw the words "bless" and "blessing" around a lot, don't we? Sometimes, when you ask someone how they're doing, they'll say, "Oh, I'm blessed." If someone sneezes, we say, "God bless you." When we're told something that's a little shocking or surprising, we say, "Well, bless my soul!" When someone recovers from an illness, we say, "What a blessing."

But what exactly does it mean to be blessed? What is the real meaning of blessing?

Here is what I believe to be a true, biblical definition of blessing. *To be blessed simply means to be on the receiving end of the tangible and intangible favor of God.*

It's not a complicated thing. Anytime we have received any good thing from God—in whatever area of life—we are blessed. We are on the receiving end of God's tangible or intangible favor.

When we say the words "blessing" or "blessed," our minds often instinctively race to the intangibles of life—health, peace, love, tranquility of the soul, et cetera.

But blessings are also tangible. They are those things which we can see, touch, taste, hear and smell. Blessings permeate our lives—in work and family and emotions and friendships and thoughts and finances; intangible and tangible.

I Will Bless You and Make You a Blessing

Abraham, the father of the Hebrew nation, was someone who was on the receiving end of the intangible and tangible favor of God in a major way.

Let's pick up his story in Genesis. God said to Abraham, "I will make you into a great nation and I will bless you; I will make your name great, and you will be a blessing. I will bless those who bless you, and whoever curses you I will curse; and all peoples on earth will be blessed through you" (Genesis 12:2-3).

Abraham was called out of his own country, out of a family of idol worshipers, to be a blessing to the entire world. He was hand-picked by God to go to a new land and become a difference-maker for the one true God. Through Abraham, the nation of Israel would be born. And through the nation of Israel, a Savior would come. And through that Savior, Jesus Christ, the entire world, including you and me, would be blessed.

But the blessings of Abraham weren't just in the spiritual, intangible realm or in the far distant future. Abraham also lived in the tangible favor of God in his own time and place because of his faithfulness, because of his obedience. He was blessed positionally, occupationally, relationally, and financially.

In Genesis 24:35 one of Abraham's servants says, " The Lord has blessed my master abundantly, and he has become wealthy. He has given him sheep and cattle, silver and gold, menservants and maidservants, and camels and donkeys."

Abraham experienced some very tangible blessings of God.

And then in the New Testament we find that those who are in Christ, those who are Christ followers, have the opportunity to participate in the blessings of Abraham.

"The promises were spoken to Abraham and to his seed. The Scripture does not say 'and to seeds,' meaning many people, but 'and to your seed,' meaning one person, who is Christ. ... If you belong to Christ, then you are Abraham's seed, and heirs according to the promise." (Galatians 3:16, 29)

What is this saying to us today? It is communicating the exciting truth that we, who are in Christ, can live in the same zone that Abraham did. Through faith, we can live in the center of the sweet spot of God's success in every area of our lives.

Receiving

In order to be on the receiving end of God's blessings, though, you have to first be blessable. You've got to be in the right position to recognize and accept God's blessings. What is the right position? It's in the zone. This may seem a little like a Catch-22 situation, but let me explain.

When you are blessable, you actually know what a blessing is when you see it. Because your heart is in tune with the generous heart of God, you recognize the blessings of God when they are presented to you. You can distinguish that the good things in your life, both intangible and tangible, are truly blessings. As a result, you reside in the zone.

Abraham was in the zone, and we can be too if can pick up on two powerful principles of zone living: receiving *and* reflecting. It's not just about receiving and getting and obtaining the blessings for ourselves. It's also about reflecting those blessings to others.

We've already discovered that being blessed means being on the receiving end of the intangible and tangible favor of God. You can see in the diagram above that I have labeled

God as the Blessor. And so, living in the zone may seem to be all about *receiving* blessings from the Blessor. The next step, however, is where the rubber meets the road. It's where you put shoe leather to the blessings you receive. It's where you discover the true meaning behind God's blessings, because it isn't all about you.

Reflecting

Abraham wasn't simply blessed by God. He realized there was more to life in the zone than receiving God's blessings. He was also a blessing to others. Don't miss that. When God blessed Abraham financially, relationally, spiritually, and in every other area of his life, Abraham turned around and reflected the generous nature of God to others. God had blessed him so

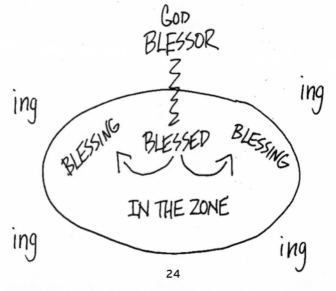

that he could be a blessing others.

Blessing is not just a figure of speech that we toss out when someone sneezes. It has great depth. And the most amazing thing about living in the zone is that it's just as available to us today as it was in Abraham's day. It didn't go out of style with rope sandals and camel's hair robes. That's why God did what he did through Christ—to give us an opportunity, like Abraham, both to be blessed and to be a blessing. God has been working overtime to get us in the zone so we can take part in the rich heritage of our great spiritual forefather, Abraham.

But we can't bless others if we haven't first been blessed. Would you like to live a life of blessing? Do you want to live in the zone? If you're a follower of Christ, you can be on the receiving end of the intangible and tangible favor of God in the same way Abraham was.

Since the nature of God is generosity and since we are made in the image of God, everything we do and are should reflect that generosity to others—emotionally, relationally, occupationally, spiritually, and yes, even financially.

We must take those blessings from God and then reflect the character of the Blessor by blessing others. Once you've become a recipient of the grace of God *and* you're reflecting the nature and character of God in every way to other people—once you've been blessed and you are a blessing—you are beginning a new life in the zone!

THE LAND OF *OR* AND THE LAND OF *ING*

Those who have taken up residence in the zone see the Blessor through the blessings they receive every day. And, because they understand where the blessings come from, they are living in the Land of OR. The Land of OR *is* the zone, because it's the Bless*or* who has given us *blessings*. Are you confused yet? Stay with me; it'll get clearer as we go along.

People in the zone recognize where their blessings come from. That's in stark contrast to those living in another place just outside the zone. That place is called the Land of ING. This zoned out wasteland represents blessing minus the "bless," leaving only the "ing." Residents of Ing never really understand the true nature of the "ings" they have been given, because they don't understand or know the Bless*or* who has given them the *blessings*. From their narrow-minded perspective, all they are able to see are the "ings."

People who live in the Land of Ing are missing out because they are zoned out. They focus so much on the ings that nothing else matters in life. All they desire, think about, and strive for are the ings—the clothe-ing, the house-ing, the bling-bling, ca-ching ca-ching! In turn, they completely ignore the Bless*or*—who is the one who gave them the ings in the first place.

In short, those living outside of the zone fail to recognize the blessings of God. They don't realize that all they have comes from God. To these people it's all about what *they* have done, what *they* have accomplished or acquired.

And as difficult as it is for me to admit, large blocks of Christians are living outside the zone and focusing on the "ings." Many of us are stumbling and fumbling the favor of God, because we aren't in the position to be blessable. Furthermore, because we aren't living the zone, in the sweet spot of God's success, we aren't able to be a blessing to others. For anyone who claims to be a follower of Christ, outside the zone is a pitiable and pathetic place to be.

Basically, when someone is zoned out, they see the Ings but they miss the Or. They have the things, the trappings of worldly success, but they aren't able to enjoy them or share them with others because they don't recognize the only One who can show them what true success is. And because they focus on the ings rather than the Or, they become eaten up with envy, jealousy, and greed—something we'll look at later in the book.

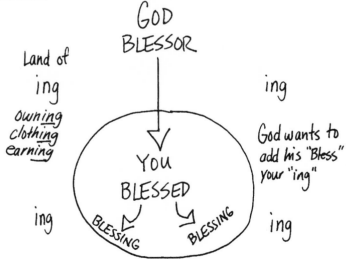

The sad reality is the residents of the Land of ING don't realize how much more God could do in and through their lives if they moved into the zone, into the Land of OR. When you move into the Land of OR, your life is catapulted to the next level. Living in the Land of OR helps you recognize and fulfill the potential that God has in store for your life. It allows God to stamp his super on your natural. Or in this context, to add his bless to your ings.

When you're in the zone, in the Land of OR, you have a "God heartedness" about you. Your finger is on his pulse. You understand and recognize what his will is for your life—which is to leverage the spiritual, relational, and material blessings he's given you to bless others for his glory. And that's how we are wired to live—zoned into that sweet spot of God's success!

Abraham's Legacy

To understand just what God-heartedness is, let's look again at the life of Abraham. Abraham clearly had a God heartedness about him that was reflected in every area of his life.

- God told him to sacrifice his first born son and he willingly obeyed. He was ready to *give* God his best. Even until the very last second, with the knife raised high and ready to strike, Abraham stayed true to God's will. And because of that faithfulness, God provided a ram at the perfect time to replace his son on the altar. This is a foreshadowing of something greater to come—the fact that through Abraham's seed, Christ would come and serve as the ultimate sacrifice for the sins of all humanity.

- Then Abraham teamed up with his nephew, Lot. The group eventually got so big that they had to split up and go separate ways. When it came time to choose which part of the land they each would claim for themselves and their people, Abraham said, "Lot, you choose first." Although Abraham had every right to choose first (as the eldest and greater of the two), he *gave* his nephew first dibs. And when Lot got into trouble in the land of Sodom, who do you think pleaded to God to rescue him? It was Abraham, of course.

- Abraham also *gave* out of his material possessions. Without being asked, he brought a gift of 10% (a tithe) of everything he had to Melchizedek, a priest and king of Salem. Because Melchizedek worshiped "God Most High" and was both a priest and king, Abraham recognized him as a priest of God and tithed to him. Melchizedek was an Old Testament representation of Jesus Christ, the ultimate High Priest and King.

How could Abraham do all these things? He lived *in the zone.* He was on the receiving end of God's intangible and tangible favor. But it didn't stop with receiving. He received it for himself (he was blessed) and then reflected it to others (he was a blessing).

MANAGEMENT VS. OWNERSHIP

Basically, God heartedness comes down to understanding the difference between management and ownership. Once Abraham was ambushed by the favor of God, once he received it, he had to reflect it. He had no choice because he understood what God's blessings were all about. The light came on in his life and he moved from being an owner to being a manager.

True success is about management, not ownership. We don't own one thing. We came into this life with nothing. We'll leave this life with nothing.

People may say, "Well, Ed, you don't understand. I've pulled myself up by the bootstraps. You don't know what I have made of my life. You don't know my background. I'm a fighter."

But I have to ask, "Who gave you your life, your creativity, your drive, and your people skills? Who gave you your intellect? Who enabled you? Who empowered you? Who blessed you?"

The answer is: God! God gave everything to us with the snap of a finger. He can take it away like that, too.

Jesus illustrated this point beautifully when he talked about the parable of the talents in Matthew 25:14-30. He told the story of a wealthy landowner who was going out of town on a business trip. This rich man entrusted his money to three servants. To the first servant he gave five talents ($4800); to one he gave two talents ($1920); and to the third he gave one talent ($960).

While the rich landowner was away, the first two servants

doubled their master's money. The one who had five talents parlayed his into ten talents. The one who had two talents parlayed his into four talents. But the one who had one talent dug a hole in the ground and just sat on the money.

Then the day of accountability arrived. The wealthy landowner came back. He said to the first two, "Men, those of you who have multiplied the talents, good for you! You were faithful over little, now I'll make you faithful over much."

To the one who dug a hole and sat on his talent the master said, "You wicked, lazy servant! So you knew that I harvest where I have not sown and gather where I have not scattered seed? Well then, you should have put my money on deposit with the bankers, so that when I returned I would have received it back with interest." He then took the talent from him and gave it to the one who had ten talents.

Jesus concluded the parable with this sobering statement: "For everyone who has will be given more, and he will have an abundance. Whoever does not have, even what he has will be taken from him. And throw that worthless servant outside, into the darkness, where there will be weeping and gnashing of teeth" (Matthew 25:29-30).

Jesus' point is clear. We are to use what he has given us to advance his work and his kingdom. As a Christ follower I am called to develop my gifts and abilities and parlay them for Christ. But that's not all.

There's another vitally important aspect to Jesus' story. I am also called to care for and invest the financial resources God has entrusted to me and give them back as an act of worship to

God. I am not supposed to take all of that stuff, dig a hole and sit on it. I'm called to utilize it. And then, as I use my gifts, abilities and money within the context of the local church, and as I give it back to God what is his, God says, "Well done. I have given you the ability to communicate. I have given you the ability to make money. I have given you the ability to work with people. I have given you the ability to organize. You have developed that and returned it as an act of worship. Well done."

There is more wealth in our nation today than ever before. But that wealth has also made people more selfish than ever before. In short, we are greedy. As our earnings have increased, our yearnings have increased. And many of us are just throwing God some pocket change here and there. We are not worshipping God with our talents as he calls us to do.

One day, though, he is going to come back and look at each of us face-to-face; and a lot of people who go by the label of "Christ followers" will hang their heads in shame because their greed and selfishness has kept them from being in the center of God's will. It has kept them out of the zone.

Money is a very personal subject, I know. It cuts to the heart of who we are. Any time I talk about money, it gets a lot of people worked up and immediately puts them on the defensive. Many people say, "Oh, here he goes talking about money again."

But little do they know that statements like that are billboard advertisements of their greed. They think they own all of their stuff. They have an ownership mentality instead of management mentality.

Generous people don't say things like that, because they

realize, "Hey, I don't have any stuff. God gave me my stuff and he owns all my stuff."

Consequently, they are very generous with what God has given them and they don't mind when I, or anyone else, talks about money management.

When we are God-hearted, we understand the fact that God owns all of the stuff and that we are just managers. And when we understand that reality, our God-heartedness will be evidenced by God generated generosity to others. When we get in on the receiving end of God's favor, we will move from an ownership mentality to a management mentality.

And once that happens, we put ourselves into a position to be blessable; and we can turn around and be a blessing to others. That's the zone!

The ownership mentality, on the other hand, is a blessing blocker. It clogs what God wants to do in and through your life. When you think your stuff is your stuff; when you think that *your* mind, *your* drive, *your* creativity and *your* ingenuity did it; you are following a guaranteed formula for frustration.

That's not the way God wants you to live. God wants to put his super on your natural. That's when you get a proper perspective or a good read on your resources, abilities and position in life. That's when you realize that God is in charge, that he is the owner and that we are simply called to steward his stuff. And that's when you move from a clog to a conduit of God's blessings.

Some of God's first instructions to Adam and Eve were all about the very issue of management. In Genesis 1:29-30 God tells Adam and Eve, "I give you every seed-bearing plant on the face of the whole earth and every tree that has fruit with seed in it. They will be yours for food. And to all the beasts of the earth and all the birds of the air and all the creatures that move on the ground-everything that has the breath of life in it-I give every green plant for food."

Those instructions had to do with stuff, material possessions, things. You can do a lot of great things in life; but if you're holding back from blessing others financially; if you're keeping from God what is already his; if you think that your stuff is your stuff and that you can do whatever you want with it, then you're not living in the zone. You're missing out on the blessings of God.

Aligning Yourself with God

Please don't misunderstand the gist of this book. I'm not saying that living in the zone has anything to do with us *making* God do things. God is not a gumball machine. Being in the zone is not about God aligning himself with your desires. On the contrary, it's all about aligning yourself with God and his desires. God does not change to bless us. In fact, God says himself in Malachi 3:6, "I the Lord do not change."

So living in the zone is all about us making the move, making the changes, to get in line with the way God wants us to live. The blessings that come to us at that point are just part of the spiritual reality of being where God wants us. The very first Psalm lays it out for us: "Blessed is the man (v. 1) …[whose] delight is in the Law of the Lord (v.2)…Whatever he does prospers" (v. 3).

When we align ourselves with him, God can bless us. And when he blesses us, we can be a blessing to others.

That's, again, why I am so excited about this topic. I want those who are zoned out—those who are stalled and paralyzed—to learn to be zoned in and reach their full potential. This book is all about helping you discover how to change and experience the blessings of God. This information can help you be all that God wants you to be. Just like when you are taught about marriage or family or dealing with fear, it's to help you excel in those areas. It's no different when you receive teaching about money.

I used to shy away from money talk because I was afraid people would take it the wrong way or that they would be offended in some way. After all, the leaders and televangelists and preachers who have abused their power and exploited people for money are plentiful. I was afraid of being grouped in with those people.

But I'm not those people. And now I love to talk about money because money is an integral part of everything in this world. My goal as a pastor and leader is simply to teach the truth of God's Word—and, as we will discover, there is plenty in God's Word about money.

IT'S ALL ABOUT THE MONEY

People say, sometimes scornfully, "It's all about the money." Well, in a manner of speaking, it *is* all about the money. That statement has ramifications from the stock market on Wall Street to the meat market in your hometown. And it is also true and powerful in God's economy as well.

Over 500 verses in the Bible talk about prayer; around 500 verses talk about faith. But more than 2,000 verses in the Bible cover the subject of money and possessions. And Jesus talked more about money than he talked about almost anything else. Of the 38 parables that Jesus told, 16 of them center on the topic of money, possessions and our responsibility with those things.

I also think it's interesting that the word "believe" is used 272 times; "pray" is used 371 times; "love" is used 714 times. But the word "give" is used 2,162 times!

That's why we can't ignore the money issue. We can't be shy about discussing something that is a central theme in the Bible.

This book is all about money management God's way, from our Maker's point of view. I realize that you get advice from a lot of different sources regarding money management—friends, family, financial gurus, television commercials and magazine articles all converge to tell us the best way for us to use our money. Too many of us, though, have never listened to the right advisor when it comes to financial matters—God.

Money is powerful, powerful stuff. It relates in some way to almost everything we do. Many people are drowning in debt. Others don't have a financial worry in the world. Some people feel guilty about the amount of money they make. And still others worship money—it fuels them, rules them and dominates them. For many, their self-esteem is determined by money. For these people, net worth and self worth are intrinsically woven together.

But no matter what financial state you find yourself in,

reading this book can be a defining moment to help you experience life in the zone.

We spend a lot of our time trying to earn, save and spend money—it's a representation of who we are. And in a very real sense, it is a piece of who we are. That's why Jesus said in Matthew 6:21, "For where your treasure is, there your heart will be also."

To live in the zone you have to put money in its proper context. But for most people, money is way out of context. And the reason is because so many of us are zoned out. To accomplish what God wants to accomplish in our lives, we must understand what to do with what God has given us. We have to zone in. Some people drift in and out of the zone, not thinking about the fact that if they made this much in disobedience, think how much more you're going to make in obedience!

Money is actually a test from God. It really reveals everything about us. If you want to find out what makes someone tick, just look at their bank account or credit card statement. People like to say that money talks. Well, what is your money saying about your life? Money reveals our priorities, loyalties and affections. In fact, how we manage it directly dictates how many blessings we will or will not experience in life. And it determines whether we are zoned in or zoned out. So read ahead as we discover some practical ways to live in the zone and truly experience the favor of God.

GET IN THE ZONE
BECOMING GOD HEARTED

- Living in the zone is first and foremost about seeing God as he really is and mimicking his character in our lives.

- To be blessed simply means to be on the receiving end of the tangible and intangible favor of God.

- In order to be on the receiving end of God's blessings you have to first be blessable.

- We must take those blessing from God and then reflect the character of the Blessor by blessing others.

- When someone is zoned out, they see the ings but they miss the Or. They have the things, the trappings of worldly success, but they aren't able to enjoy them or share them with others because they don't recognize the Blessor

- God heartedness comes down to understanding the difference between management and ownership.

- We are to use what he has given us to advance his work and his kingdom.

- As I use my gifts, abilities and money within the context of the local church, and as I give back to God what is his, God says, "Well done."

- Being in the zone is not about God aligning himself with your desires. It's all about aligning yourself with God and his desires.

Ephesians 5:1   "Be imitators of God."

CHAPTER TWO
SKITTLES®

A while back I took my family to a high school football game. During the middle of the third quarter, one of my twin daughters came to me and asked for some money to buy some candy. Normally I don't buy a lot of candy for my kids, but I handed her a $5 bill and told her she could have some. She made her way to the concession stand and came back with a package of Skittles. As she was eating the Skittles I asked her, "Landra, can I have a few Skittles?"

She looked at her Skittles, then looked back at me and said, "No!"

Landra didn't understand several realities. Number one, she didn't understand that if had I wanted to, I could have forcibly taken the Skittles from her and eaten every one myself. She didn't realize the strength I have.

Number two, she didn't understand that I was the one who actually bought them for her. She paid for them with *my* money.

Number three, she didn't understand that if I had wanted to, I could have bought her so many packages of Skittles that she couldn't even eat them all.

The same realities apply to our lives as well. God has given all of us some Skittles. He looks at you and me and he says, "I'd like some Skittles. Would you give me some Skittles? I just want a few back."

But many of us defiantly say, "No, God! They're mine." And God says again, "Can I have some Skittles?"

But we still respond, "No. They're mine."

Like my daughter Landra, many of us don't understand three things. Number one, if God wanted to, he could take all of our Skittles from us. We forget that he's much stronger than we are.

Number two, we fail to realize that God is the one who gave us the Skittles in the first place.

And number three, if God wanted to, he could rain so many Skittles on our lives that we wouldn't know what to do with them all.

In the first chapter we discovered that the zone is the sweet spot of God's success. It is the blessed place where God wants all of us to live. In this chapter, we are going to learn that God has given each of us a certain amount of resources. And what we do with those resources relates directly to whether we live in the zone or out of the zone. What we do with our resources, our Skittles, determines whether we're zoned in or zoned out.

We also saw the first glimpse of a recurring theme for this book—God is for us. God wants us to live in the sweet spot of his success. He wants to bless your life and mine. The word blessing simply means to be on the receiving end of the intangible and tangible favor of God.

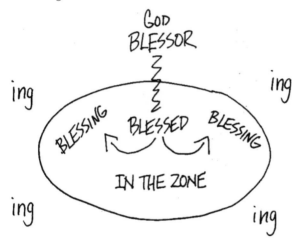

Take another look at the diagram above, the same one I showed you in the last chapter. God is the Blessor. And as the Blessor, he gives us blessings, which are his tangible and intangible favor. And when we receive the tangible and intangible blessings from his hand and then, in turn, reflect God's character by becoming a blessing, we are living in the zone.

But there's a hard reality to life in the zone. Only about 21% of Christians are living in the zone. 79% of Christians are out of the zone. The 79-percenters are into the own-ing, the clothe-ing, the house-ing, the bling-bling, and the ca-ching, ca-ching. They don't recognize that everything comes from the Blessor. They have the ings without the bless. And because of that, because they don't recognize the Blessor, they are not truly blessed. And because they are not receiving God's blessings, they cannot reflect those blessings to others.

One of the very tangible aspects of God's blessing is the fact that we each have stuff, money. We all have a bunch of Skittles. Some of us have huge piles of Skittles. Others have a medium sized pile. And still others have a small pile of Skittles. But no matter how big our pile of Skittles is, our management of what God has entrusted to us has monstrous implications on whether or not we are living in the zone.

If we're zoned out, we think we are the owners. However, if we're zoned in, we realize that we're managers. When we are God-hearted, as we discovered in the first chapter, we understand that God owns all of our stuff. God owns all of our Skittles. As we move to that area of understanding, then our God-heartedness is evidenced by our God-generated generosity to others. When we get in gear with that, *then* we get in on the receiving end of God's favor. Positionally, we're in the right spot to be blessable and to turn around and be a blessing.

In this chapter, I want us to zone in on several things. In fact, what I want to unpack and explain is probably the quickest route for the 79-percenters to experience life in the zone. And it has to do with money management.

MONEY MATTERS

What does money management have to do with living in the zone, in the sweet spot of God's success? The reason we talk about money management is because money represents who we are. We spend a lot of our time in this life making money, spending money, investing money, saving money, and for some of us, wasting money.

The question is: *Are you who you are because of what you have? Or do you have what you have because of who you are?* In other words, does your money manage you or do you manage your money?

Because money represents so much of our lives, it determines in a profound way whether we are zoned in or zoned out in God's economy. That's why I want to help you in this whole arena of money management. Money, and specifically money management, touches in one way or another everything in this world.

If you're thinking at this point, "So is this whole chapter about giving?" Well, yes and no. I am talking about giving. But it goes much deeper than that. This chapter is not really about giving as much as it is about honoring God.

Proverbs 3:9 says, "Honor the Lord with your wealth, with the firstfruits of all your crops."

It's very simple. If you don't understand biblical money management then you're not going to know what it means to honor God. And if you don't understand how to honor God, you aren't living in the zone.

I have to ask again, "What is your money saying about your life?" Because, what you do with your money is directly related to how many blessings you will or will not receive and experience in your life. And nowhere is this truer than with the biblical concept of the tithe.

The Tithe

The tithe seems to be a mysterious, even scary concept for many people. But the word tithe simply means one-tenth. There's nothing religious about that term. It is just a numerical term meaning one-tenth, or ten percent. When the word tithe is used in the Bible, it simply refers to bringing the first ten percent of our income or gain back to God.

Malachi 3:10 spells it out for us in very basic terms. "'Bring the whole tithe into the storehouse, that there may be food in my house. Test me in this,' says the Lord Almighty, 'and see if I will not throw open the floodgates of heaven and pour out so much blessing that you will not have room enough for it.'"

The principle of tithing goes all the way back to the beginning of creation. God told Adam and Eve in Genesis 2:15 to take care of the garden, to manage the garden. Then he said in verse 17, "One tree. I'm going to keep one tree for me. You can enjoy the rest of paradise, but don't touch that one tree."

When he created the world in 6 days and rested on the seventh, he set an example for us: "Work six days. But on the seventh day rest; set aside that one day for me." In the Ten Commandments he told the Israelites, "Remember the Sabbath Day and keep it holy" (Exodus 20:8).

When Israel entered the Promised Land, there were ten cities that needed to be conquered. God said, "Take all of the spoils from the first city that you conquer, all of the gold and the silver, and bring it to my house."

All of these are biblical examples of setting apart the best for God, which is foundational to the principle of tithing to him what belongs to him.

Bring It in Faith

As we consider the concept of the tithe within the entire context of Scripture, we have to look at the biblical principle of the first born. In Exodus 13:2, "God says to consecrate to me all of the first born. Whatever opens the womb among the children of Israel birthed of man and beast, it is mine."

Here God says that the first born is his. It belongs to him. God declares sixteen times in the Bible that the first born is his. So every time someone's livestock delivered its first born, they were to either sacrifice it; or, if it was unclean, they had to redeem it with a clean, spotless lamb.

When the first born lamb came into the world, you didn't wait and let your ewe produce nine more lambs and then give God the next one. God says, "Give the first one." It requires faith to give the first one. The first portion is packed with power. When the first portion is brought back to God, the rest is blessed.

In today's world, we are called to bring our tithes, or the first fruits of our labor, in the same way. We have to bring it *before* we see the blessings of God. And to do that we have to bring it in faith. Tithing is simply saying, "I'm going to bring it to you first, God, and trust you to bless the rest."

The same is true of our time. You come to church on the first day of the week, and that is the way of giving God the firstfruits of your time. You give God the first of your time and he is going to bless the rest of the week. If you don't, it's not going to happen for you.

Some people view Monday as the beginning of the week and they give the first part of their week to making money. Others think the week begins on Friday and they give the first part of their week to recreation. For them, it's all about the weekend.

As God's people, we need to give the first part of our week to Jesus. The reason the New Testament church met on Sunday was because they were celebrating the resurrection, which occurred on the first day of the week. That doesn't mean you can't worship on Saturday evening. The principle is the same. You are setting aside that time to honor God.

The recurring idea in all of these instances is that God asks people to honor him in faith with the first part of everything he's given us.

Fundamentally throughout Scripture, however, the tithe is not referring to time or talent as much as it is to treasure. God knew that money was going to be important to us. So the tithe is really all about the mean green. The first born belonged to God. And also, the firstfruits belonged to him.

In Exodus 23:19 (NKJV) we read, "The first of the firstfruits of your land you shall bring into the house of the Lord your God."

Because of the first of your firstfruits is what God wants, it means the last of your firstfruits isn't acceptable. That portion is not going to cut it. It's not just any tenth portion of your firstfruits. The tithe is the *first* tenth of your firstfruits.

Bring It to The Proper Place

The above passage also talks about bringing the tithe to the proper place. It says "...to the house of the Lord your God." It doesn't say to give to a Christian school. It doesn't say to give to a missionary organization. It doesn't say to give to a para-church group. The tithe belongs to the local house of worship, the local church. Whatever church you call your home church is where your tithe belongs.

Some people say, "Well, you know, I'll give maybe five percent to a missionary. I'll give two percent to a Christian school or university. And the rest I'll give to my church."

That's not the tithe. It's important to support missionaries. It's important to support Christian academic institutions. I believe very strongly in supporting various ministries. My wife and I are completely supportive of other Christian organizations. In fact, our children go to a Christian school that we contribute to financially. Those contributions, though, should be over and above the ten percent that we bring into the local church. The local church is most near and dear to the heart of God; that is where the tithe belongs.

The Bible doesn't say to give the first of your firstfruits to any organization you want. It says to bring the first of the firstfruits into "the house of the Lord your God." We must always bring it to God's house first. After that, we are free to give generously to wherever we want.

Think about the implications. The church is the heartbeat of God. When my three daughters get married, I'm not going to go to a missionary or to a Christian university for their wedding. I'm going to the local church. When loved ones pass away, we go to the local church. When we have a spiritual need, it's the local church we turn to.

One of the greatest things about bringing the tithe to the local church is this. God is going to bless his church, we know that. But how does God bless his church? By blessing the people in the church! God blesses people in the church musically, artistically, and intellectually. But God is also going to bless the people in the church financially in order to finance the church.

For some reason, Christians often have a hard time accepting the fact that God wants to bless his people financially. But how else is he going bankroll the work of the church except by blessing the people in the church financially.

Look again at Proverbs 3:9-10, "Honor the Lord with your wealth, with the firstfruits of all your crops; then your barns will be filled to overflowing, and your vats will brim over with new wine."

During the writing of this text, the majority of people were farmers. They raised animals and grew crops. Increase came as their crops were harvested and livestock reproduced.

Today, you might be a teacher, a banker, a pastor, a real estate executive, a coach, or a construction worker and your increase comes in those venues. As you make a regular income or as you realize any gain on your income or investments, you need to honor God with the first part of that.

Bring It to God

Have you noticed in all of the Scripture we've seen so far related to the tithe that the word "bring" is used. It's important to emphasize that we don't give the tithe. We *bring* it to the local church.

Tithing is bringing back to God what is already his. We set it aside first because it already belongs to him. He owns everything anyway, but he just asks that we bring back to him the first tenth, the first ten percent, of what he has blessed us with.

Whenever we think we give a tithe, we're out of sync with God's plan. We are not aligned with him, in the zone. The word give relates to ownership, not management. We think the money is ours to give to God. In reality, it is his money that we are bringing back to him.

Usually at Christmastime, my wife and I give some money to our kids to go buy Christmas presents. They wouldn't have any money unless we gave it to them, so we give them some cash to do a little shopping for their friends and family. And we get a lot of enjoyment out of watching our kids buy those gifts with our money. It's really enjoyable, though, to watch them give a gift to us purchased with our own money, with some of the money we gave them in the first place. That's a whole other level of enjoyment—and not just because we got a gift or two. Our joy comes from the fact that our children were bringing to us, out of honor and love, a part of what we had given to them.

God is the same way. He gives us some cash, some stuff, and he asks us to bring a portion back to him. By doing that we are not only putting ourselves in a position to be blessed by him, we are also demonstrating our love for him and honoring him. Just as our children bring us a lot of joy at Christmas, when we faithfully bring, not give, the whole tithe to our heavenly Father's house, it brings him a lot of joy as well.

Blessings or Curses

Do you remember the classic biblical story of Joshua fighting the battle of Jericho? Well, there's a part of the story you may not remember. God gave Joshua strict instructions that the Israelites were not to keep any of the spoils from Jericho. God told him that none of it belonged to the people. It was all God's.

Why did God say all the silver and gold from Jericho had to be given to the Lord's house? It was because Jericho was the first city conquered in the Promised Land. Again, it was the firstfruits.

God was saying, "Bring all the silver and gold from Jericho into my house. *Then* you can have all the rest." He didn't say, "Conquer ten cities and give me all the spoils from the tenth one." He said, "Give me the first, and you can have the rest."

This account, though, also mentions a little known person named Achan. Achan was a man who disrespected God. The people were told specifically that the silver and gold from Jericho were consecrated to the Lord because it was his. But Achan decided that he couldn't resist the temptation to take some for himself. You read in Joshua 7 that the gold and silver that Achan took was cursed.

Think about that. When the spoils were given to God as he commanded, they were consecrated. They were blessed.

They were set apart. But when Achan decided to take some for himself, it was cursed.

The tithe, 10%, is consecrated to the Lord and to the Lord's house because it is his. But if we take it for ourselves, it becomes cursed because it's stolen. We are stealing from God.

Would you rather try to make it through life with 100% of your income that is cursed? Or would you rather try to make it through life with 90% of your income blessed by God?

Now you might be saying, "That's pretty harsh."

Well, Malachi says if we keep the tithe to ourselves we're robbing God. We looked earlier at Malachi 3:10. But check out the two verses preceding that.

Malachi 3:8-9, "Will a man rob God? Yet you rob me. But you ask, 'How do we rob you?' in tithes and offerings. You are under a curse—the whole nation of you—because you are robbing me."

Some people try to overlook this Scripture and dismiss it, "Well, that's in the Old Testament. Tithing is just an old concept that doesn't apply today." In the very same chapter of Malachi, though, God says, "I the Lord do not change."

OLD COVENANT VS. NEW COVENANT

If you think the principle of the tithe is no longer active, here's my question to you. When God declares, "I do not change," then when did these things supposedly change? When did God change?

You cannot dismiss the tithe.

The tithe all belongs to God. It's an unchanging principle

established by an unchanging God.

Some argue, "Well, tithing was under the Law, so I don't have to do it. We're under grace now." But this whole principle of a tithe was introduced long before the Law in the Old Testament ever came into existence.

The principle of the tithe predates the Law of Moses by hundreds of years. It was in operation as Abraham was asked to sacrifice his first son, Isaac. There was much more at stake than just money. Abraham was asked to offer up his first born son. But Abraham had faith. He didn't wait to see if he was going to have ten sons before he gave his first son. Nor did God go to Abraham when he only had Isaac and say, "Hey, after you've had four or five more sons I'm going to come back to you and ask you for one of them." No. God asked for the first one when that was all Abraham had.

It was in operation when Abraham gave a tenth of his income to the high priest Melchizedek. And just as Abraham did, we are to give a tenth of our income to Christ who, the book of Hebrews says, is the great High Priest in the order of Melchizedek.

The principle of tithing goes all the way back to God accepting Abel's offering and rejecting Cain's offering. Cain brought an offering of some of his fruit over an extended period of time. Abel, though, brought the first born of his flock. God accepted Abel's offering. Yet, he denied Cain's offering. The Bible says in the process of time, Cain grew his crops. But he didn't give the firstfruits. He gave a few pieces of fruit here and there—when it was convenient.

It even goes back further to when God gave Adam and Eve instructions about setting apart the Tree of the Knowledge of Good and Evil in the Garden of Eden. The first sentence God spoke to Adam and Eve had to do with stewardship. Yet, by choosing to eat the fruit, Adam and Eve failed to follow God's instructions. They acted like they owned the garden, when in reality they were only called to manage the garden.

Even as we consider the relationship of the tithe to the Law of Moses, there were many things that were under the Law that continue to be principles of God under grace. Consider adultery. It would be absurd for someone to argue, "Hey, you know, adultery was forbidden under the Law. But I guess now it's acceptable because we're under grace."

Or think of someone defending robbery by saying, "You know, stealing was forbidden under the Law. But now it's okay under grace, right? After all, we're under the new covenant!"

Just because tithing was an Old Testament principle does not mean that it isn't still applicable. The principle of tithing is biblical and eternal.

In the New Testament, Paul told the Corinthian Church in 1 Corinthians 16:1-2, "Now about the collection for God's people: Do what I told the Galatian churches to do. On the first day of every week, each one of you should set aside a sum of money in keeping with his income...."

What were they doing? They were setting apart the portion of their income that belonged to God. All the money is God's, but Paul was instructing them to bring back to God the portion that God had asked them to set aside for his church.

Paul says we're to give every week on the first day of the week—as God has prospered us. We should give to God first in direct proportion to the size of our paychecks and any other financial gain.

Is it really an act of faith to give 10% only after all your other bills are paid? What does it say about our priorities if we pay all of our bills first and then give whatever pocket change is left over to God?

If you want to be zoned in, if you want to experience life in the blessed place, that first portion is the one that blesses the rest. The first portion carries the blessing.

People may claim, "Yeah, God is number one in my life. He's first. Jesus is Lord of my life."

But talk is cheap. Tithing is the litmus test that tests whether we are willing to put our money where our mouth is. It is a tangible witness that God is first. If you say that God is first in your life, prove it in your checkbook. That's where the rubber meets the road.

Again, I'm not talking about tithing because God needs the money. I'm delivering these truths for your own sake. God doesn't need you to give. He asks you to honor him so that he can bless your life. I've never met someone who tithed regularly who was not blessed. For God not to bless your life as you are faithful to his commands would go against his unchanging nature.

He asks you to bring the tithe because he is on your side. Remember, God is for you, not against you. I'm going to keep reiterating that theme until it's tattooed on your heart. God desperately wants you to live in the zone, and the only way that's going to happen is if you honor God with the first part of your wealth.

The Treasure Test

Jesus said in Matthew 6:21, "For where your treasure is, there your heart will be also."

Our treasure is tethered to our heart. The simple reason people get irritated with me when I talk about money is this: *I've told them where their heart is.*

Most people would rather not know where their heart is. It's a subject most of us try to avoid. But, if we want to live life in the favor of God, in the zone of the sweet spot of God's success, it's an issue we all must face.

Jesus did not say, "Where your heart is, there your treasure will be." No. It tells us that our heart follows our treasure. Feelings follow actions; actions don't follow feelings. If you are waiting for your heart to get in the right place; if you are waiting for a certain feeling or a quiver in your liver before you start tithing, you're never going pass the treasure test.

By the way, there's no way to cheat on this test. You can't negotiate your way out. God's not into the negotiating business. We don't say, "Hey, God, how about 3%," and then he says, "How about 7%," just for us to come back with, "Okay...5%, and that's my final offer."

No. We need to bring the whole tithe.

The only place in the Bible where it says to test God is over the issue of the tithe. In Malachi 3:10, God says, "Test me in this." Are you ready to put God to the test? If you are, then get ready for the floodgates of heaven to open in your life.

If I tithe, I'm blessed. If I don't, I'm cursed. It's not a very difficult decision, really. Blessing or cursing? You make the call.

Raising The Bar

Every time Christ points to the Old Covenant, he sets a higher standard. He raises the bar under the New Covenant of grace. We see this especially in Matthew 5:17-20.

The law said, "Don't murder." Christ comes along, though, and says, "Don't even hold a grudge." The New Covenant holds us to a higher standard.

The law says, "Don't commit adultery." But Christ says, "Don't even look lustfully at a woman." Again, it's a higher standard.

The level of righteousness that grace demands goes much further than the law demands. People will sometimes say, "I don't tithe because I'm not under law. I'm under grace."

I say, "Great! That means you should be giving a lot more than 10%, because the righteousness of grace always exceeds the righteousness of law."

Think about how our perspective of tithing will change when we begin to see the local church as a visible manifestation of God's love. Christ has gone away for a season. And I believe he is saying to us, "While I'm away, I want each of you to take care of my bride. Bring the tithe into the storehouse."

When I shared Landra's Skittles story for the first time in our church, I got a letter a few days later with an empty package of Skittles in it. And inside the empty package was a check for $80,000! Attached to the package was a note that simply said, "Dear Ed, Here are some of our Skittles that we want to bring back to God."

Now, that doesn't happen all the time. What that couple did was an amazing act of faith on their part. They recognized that the local church is the heartbeat of God. They recognized that they needed to step out and give to his church. They understood that God had given them a pile of Skittles and that they had a responsibility to bring some back. For that couple, it wasn't all about what *they* had done, what *they* had accumulated or what *they* possessed. They knew that the pile of Skittles in their life wasn't about them at all. It was all about God.

They are part of the 21-percenters that I mentioned earlier in the chapter, because they did something that only about 21% of the church does: they tithed. Statistically, about 79% of those who attend church on a regular basis do not tithe to the church; they do not give ten percent of their income and gain back to God's work. Do you want to be a 79-percenter living outside the zone? Or do you want to be a 21-percenter, living inside the zone of God's tangible and intangible favor? The choice is yours.

As we segue into other aspects of money management throughout the rest of the book, don't forget what comes first. Put God first, remember the tithe, and the rest of it will fall into place. Materialism, greed, envy, debt, and every other money issue hinges on this critical issue of bringing first to God what is his. When you do that, and only when you do that, will you be able to get the rest of your financial house in order.

GET IN THE ZONE
BRINGING BACK YOUR SKITTLES

- God has given each of us a certain amount of resources. And what we do with those resources relates directly to whether we live in the zone or out of the zone.

- The question is: Are you who you are because of what you have? Or do you have what you have because of who you are?

- The idea is that God asks people to honor him with the first part of everything he's given us in faith.

- Tithing is bringing back to God what is already his. We set it aside first because it already belongs to him.

- Would you rather try to make it through life with 100% of your income that is cursed? Or would you rather try to make it through life with 90% of your income blessed by God?

- Just because tithing was an Old Testament principle does not mean that it isn't still applicable. The principle of tithing is biblical and it is eternal.

- If you want to be zoned in, if you want to experience life in the blessed place, that first portion is the one that blesses the rest.

- Put God first, remember the tithe, and the rest of it will fall into place.

Proverbs 3:9   "Honor the Lord with your wealth, with the firstfruits of all your crops."

CHAPTER THREE
CONSTRUCTION ZONE

Materialism begins where your income ends. Think about that statement for a second. Materialism begins where your income ends.

Let me ask you several questions to make that statement a little clearer. Which zip code or address makes a person materialistic? Which make and model of car? Which designer label? What vacation destination? What size home, portfolio, income or karat of diamond crosses the line into materialism?

Those are not easy questions to answer, because I suspect each person would answer that question relative to their income. That's why I can confidently say that materialism begins where our income ends.

Your perception of who is materialistic and who isn't depends on your own income. The materialistic person in your mind is rarely, if ever, in your income bracket. It's the person in the next income bracket or above. If you make $30,000, you think the person making $60,000 struggles with materialism because they have more buying power. If you make $1 million, you think the $5 million man or woman is materialistic because they are a serious power broker, financially speaking.

For most of us, that is the definition of materialism that we work with as we compare and contrast ourselves with others. But, as we will discover, there is more confusion, there are more misconceptions about materialism than almost any other subject. That's why in this chapter we're going to look at what God says about this thing called materialism.

Let me make another statement that I'll unpack over the coming pages:

Materialism is not defined by a tangible commodity, but rather by an intangible condition of the heart.

As I've said several times, money is a powerful, powerful thing. It represents who we are. It's a piece of us, a slice of our self. Because we spend so much time and energy trying to make it, save it, invest it and spend it; money is a part of us. Money is so mesmerizing that it can, if left unchecked, become your master. It wants to rule us and dominate us. Money is looking for servants. It's seeking worshippers. Our goods can quickly become our gods.

There's a deceptive side to money, however, that most of us miss. Money always over-promises and under-delivers. It promises us those things that only God can give—security, significance, identity, independence and freedom. But it always leaves us asking for more.

One place that Jesus talked about money is in Matthew 6:24. He said, "No one can serve two masters. Either he will hate the one and love the other, or he will be devoted to the one and despise the other. You cannot serve both God and money."

Jesus was basically saying that no one can have two bosses. The business world didn't come up with that philosophy. Jesus did. It would be mass confusion if, in the professional world, you had to directly report to and serve two different bosses with two different philosophies of business.

From a spiritual standpoint, the same is true. All of us must choose whom we will serve. We can either choose to serve ourselves in the Land of Ing by pursuing wealth, materialism and selfish pleasures. Or we can choose to serve God by managing our money according to his instructions.

Christ was saying that we can only have one master. But we live in a materialistic society where many Christians try to serve God and money at the same time. They spend their entire lives collecting, storing it, investing it and spending it—basically doing deals—and then dying and leaving it behind. Their desire for money and what it can buy far outweighs their commitment to God in spiritual matters.

I Timothy 6:10 warns, "The love of money is the root of all kinds of evil."

Notice that verse doesn't say that money is the root of all evil. It says the *love* of money is the root of all kinds of evil. In other words, money should serve us. We shouldn't serve money.

One of the most dangerous things about money is that if we love it, it will lead us. On the other hand, if we lead it, it will serve us. If we love money instead of leading it, instead of leveraging it for Christ's kingdom, it will keep us zoned out.

Money has the potential to be used for good or bad, for righteousness or unrighteous acts, for the temporal or eternal purposes.

And one of the main reasons the enemy works so hard to confuse us and to mess us up concerning money is the fact that, if we have the right view of it, our lives will be more effective for God. He knows the more money, for example, we give to the church, the more people will become Christ followers. The more we give to the church, the more marriages will be unified. Fragmented families will come together. More students will live for the Lord. More people will overcome substance abuse. And many more men and women will conquer the sin of lust.

How we use our money can simultaneously diminish the evil one's dominion and make us more like our heavenly Father. That's why Satan doesn't give up easily when it comes to money matters.

SATAN'S HIGHWAYS

No matter what city you live in, there is probably one thing you can always count on—highway construction. Whether it's the 105 in L.A., I-10 in Houston, the Dallas North Tollway, the Tri-State Tollway in Illinois or the Palmetto Expressway in Florida, highway construction seems to be everywhere.

We aren't the only ones into construction, though. Satan is in the highway construction business as well. And he has built a couple of highways from the edge of the zone that launch us into the Land of Ing.

These two freeways that attack our hearts and minds come from opposite mentalities, but they have one thing in common. They're both centered on material possessions. And they are both designed to keep us zoned out.

The Guilt Trip

If we take the first highway Satan builds, we end up going on a guilt trip. I also call this the "poor boy" mentality. When we take this highway out of the zone, it causes us to be ashamed of the blessings of God.

It's very ironic. If you are in the zone you realize that God is the owner, you are the manager and that you are blessed. But when you get onto the guilt trip highway, you begin to feel ashamed and guilt-ridden because of those very blessings.

We've already established that being obedient to God, being a giver, bringing the tithe, and being generous with your talent and your time and your abilities will result in God's blessings (remember, blessings are intangible *and* tangible). And, while the evil one can't stop those blessings from coming, he can try to make you ashamed of it.

Let me ask you a question: Is there anything God could do in your life for which you should feel ashamed?

Is there a tangible or intangible gift that should make us hang our head? Of course not! We have to understand the fact that doing things God's way, being obedient to God, and being in the zone will result in blessings. So often, people in the zone feel as though they have to apologize for what God has given them. Don't ever do that!

Just remember this: our forgiving God is also *for giving.* Don't be ashamed of the things he's given to you.

If you are blessed financially, or in some other realm of your life, someone at some point is going to say this to you, "Well, it must be nice." I encourage you to respond this way, "Yes, it is. God has really blessed me." And leave it at that.

Don't let anyone shame you or cause you to second-guess God's hand of blessing in your life. You know that you have been faithful to God with your financial resources, gifts, talents and abilities. And God knows it too. So, don't let other people's petty jealousies keep you from enjoying what God has so graciously given you to enjoy.

The Ride of Pride

Another highway that Satan builds leads us down the ride of pride. Pride says, *"You* built the company, *you* had the idea, *you* earned your stuff. You're brilliant, you're fast, you're quick, and you're beautiful. And everything you have is *yours."*

And because of that mindset, we become proud of the blessings that we've received. We may have started as a manager, understanding that God owns everything and we are just stewards of his stuff. But on the ride of pride, management seductively segues into ownership and we begin to think we own it all. We move from being the leader of money to a lover of money.

The Bible tells us that pride goes before a fall. Nowhere is that truer than in the realm of money and materialism. If you are riding on Satan's freeway of pride, get ready for a fall. It is coming, sooner or later.

It's amazing how the guilt trip and ride of pride work from opposite ends of the spectrum, yet they share one commonality. They both cause us to take our focus off of God and place it on the ings, on the stuff in our lives.

Here's a question that can perhaps clarify the difference between these two road trips: What's your knee jerk reaction when someone compliments you on your watch or your outfit?

The guilt trip, poor boy mentality says, "Oh, this watch? Someone gave it to me. I didn't buy it myself." Or, "It's nothing. I got it on sale at Wal-Mart. It's just a knockoff."

The ride of pride says, "Oh, you're talking about *this* outfit? It's from Italy. It's Prada® or Chanel®. It was *very* expensive."

When we're on the ride of pride, we want people to think we paid more than we did. When someone pulls up beside you in a less expensive car, the pride trip says, "Your car is *way* better than their car."

Conversely, when we're on the guilt trip, we want others to think we paid less. Someone might pull up beside you in a more expensive car, and your poverty mentality causes you to say, "What a waste! He's probably a crook."

The poor boy mentality pushes us to justify our purchases, possessions, abilities or talents because we somehow equate blessing with evil. I can't let you think I spent very much money on anything, because that would mean I'm not spiritual.

Do you see the trap? If you've been blessed by God because you've done things his way, stop feeling guilty. Don't be ashamed of having a heart God can bless.

Over the years, God has shown me how prevalent this guilt trip mentality was in my own way of thinking. It was especially strong because I've been in and around the ministry my whole life. I grew up in a pastor's home, and everybody *knows* that ministers are supposed to be poor, right? You know the old saying in churches, "Lord, you keep him humble and we'll keep him poor."

It's staggering how many Christ followers feel like they must explain away anything good or nice in their lives. If anybody at anytime compliments them on something, they feel compelled to justify it.

But I learned a long time ago that you don't have to justify your purchases to anyone but God. If God gives you peace about purchasing something, don't worry about what someone else thinks about it. We're spending, saving, giving and bringing for an audience of one.

Again, God uses the material possessions he's given us to test us. He also uses other people's possessions to test us. In other words, how we respond to someone else being blessed says a lot about the condition of our hearts.

If we are zoned in, we don't care what other people think. We only care about what God thinks. When we are in the zone, we don't look outside of the zone for approval. We only look to the Blessor. Because when we place ourselves before God, we only compare ourselves to God's grace and God's generosity. And when we do that, all we can say is, "Thank you."

When we compare what we've done for God (which is nothing) with what God has done for us (which is everything), our heart naturally overflows with gratitude.

The flipside of that is the love of money, which ushers in selfishness, not gratitude. And selfishness is your enemy.

Have you ever looked really closely at the word "selfish"? You see the word "self" and the word "fish." So, we might conclude: if you worry about your *self*, you end up smelling like a *fish*.

Selfishness always tries to manipulate and make deals with God. We're natural born takers. We are selfish from the word go. The first words we latch onto as little children are: *I, me, my, mine*. And this preoccupation with personal pronouns always leads to a materialistic mentality. And we struggle with that our entire lives.

In the remainder of the chapter, we're going to focus on how to break free of this struggle, how to be released from the materialistic mentality.

The Twin Engines

This materialistic mentality is really driven by two twin engines—envy and greed. According to I Samuel 2:7-8, Proverbs 10:4, Proverbs 10:22 and Proverbs 11:25, wealth is a blessing from God and a byproduct of things such as obedience and generosity.

Why, then, would we put down someone whom God has blessed? Why would we consider something that came from the hand of God to be evil or shameful? The answers are envy and greed.

Many of the people in the Bible, godly men and women, were heavy hitters financially. So we need to examine our hearts, including our feelings, toward those who seem to live extravagantly by our standards today. Remember the statement at the beginning of this chapter? Materialism begins where our income ends. We don't pin the label of materialism on another person within our income range, do we? Our tendency is to call someone materialistic who has more than we do, who is in the next income bracket above us. But that's not the proper attitude we should have toward others who have more than we do.

Years ago I met someone who has a house made of rare and priceless materials. His foundation has precious stones in it. His driveway is actually made of gold. And the gates around his home are made of pearls. That sounds extravagant compared to most of our standards, doesn't it?

Who is this unbelievably wealthy person? You know him, too. I'm talking about God.

Would you say that God is materialistic? Would you say that God has a problem in this area? Of course not! And yet, he is wealthy beyond our wildest imagination and he gives freely to us out of his heavenly riches.

So the problem with materialism is not how much we have. The problem is how we think about money and how we feel about those who have more of it than we do.

Perfumania

One day a Christ-follower named Mary (not Jesus' mother) took a pound of very costly perfume and anointed Jesus' feet. After doing so, Judas, one of Christ's disciples went on tilt and said, "You could sell that perfume and give all the money to the poor! That's more than a year's salary" (John 12:1-6).

Why did Mary give such an extravagant gift? After all, it was basically the equivalent of an entire year's wages. Couldn't she have given something much less expensive? And why did this thing seem to bother Judas so much? After all, it wasn't his money. It comes down to the materialistic mentality.

Mary's generous act bothered Judas because Judas was in charge of the offerings that people gave to Christ's ministry. He wanted that money to go into the box that he controlled. Why? He was a thief. He wanted the money for his own selfish self. John 12:6 tells us that, as Christ's treasurer, Judas would often help himself to the money. This account shows us that whenever there is an act of generosity, you'll always find self-ishness battling against it.

Judas didn't really care for the poor. He didn't care that Mary wasn't giving to the poor. He was a thief. Judas pretended to be thinking about others while he was really thinking of no one but himself.

But before you judge Judas too quickly, think of your own life. This is a tactic that many of us use. It's a smoke screen: one of the oldest cover up for selfishness known to man.

When you drive by someone's house, see someone cruise around in an expensive car, or see someone's designer watch do you ever say, "Wow, that's a little extravagant! They should sell that and give the money to the poor"?

Or we may say things like, "How could anyone in good conscience drive a car that expensive?" "She could have helped a lot of people out for what she spent on those earrings," Or, "I could sure do a lot of good with the money they spent on that."

We may not say things like that out loud, but we think them just the same. And yet, while we criticize how others spend their money, we are living in a nice house, driving a nice car and wearing jewelry that may seem extravagant to someone who makes less than we do. Often, when we make those comments, we have no intention of selling *our* home, *our* car, or *our* stuff to give it to the poor. We just expect others to do it.

The bottom line is, when we make such statements it isn't because we care about the poor. We just resent the fact that someone has a nicer house, car or jewelry. It's materialism at its worst.

These kinds of remarks and thoughts only advertise that we have a mindset and heart condition of materialism. They are nothing more than envy and greed dressed up in pseudo-spiritual packaging. When we say things like that, we are revealing the true condition of our hearts.

Do you see that materialism is not a tangible commodity and is, instead an intangible condition of the heart?

You saw the true condition of Judas' heart in this exchange with Mary and Jesus. From his selfish perspective he saw a year's wages being wasted instead of passing through his money box where he could pilfer a good chunk of it.

No matter how you try to cover the odor, the stinky fish always swims back to the self. And you know when someone is swimming with the self fish because they continually try to get the focus off of their own selfishness and onto the so-called "extravagance" of others.

Selfishness hides within critical comments. It drives by nice homes and criticizes other people's blessings. Selfishness always protects the self by wagging fingers of criticism and shame at someone else. It takes the spotlight off of our own materialism and shines it on someone else simply as a diversion.

GOD'S BRIDGES

So Satan builds highways to get us out of the zone—the guilt trip and the ride of pride. But Satan is not the only one in the construction business. While Satan is constructing highways leading out of the zone, God is building bridges to bring us back to the zone, back to the blessed place. And these bridges traverse high above the evil one's freeways.

Contentment

The first bridge is contentment. It is developing the ability to admire without the need to acquire. We should be able to look at something and complement it without having to own it. Basically, that means we need to learn the secret of contentment. Yes, contentment is something we learn.

Paul tells us in Philippians 4:11-13, "Not that I speak in regard to need, for *I have learned* in whatever state I am, to be content: I know how to be abased, and I know how to abound. Everywhere and in all things I have learned both to be full and to be hungry, both to abound and to suffer need. I can do all things through Christ who strengthens me."

This bridge will specifically help break the back of envy in our lives. Envy energizes a lack of contentment; whereas, contentment drains the power of envy.

I Peter 2:1-2 (NKJV) the apostle wrote, "Laying aside all ... envy ... as newborn babes, desire the pure milk of the word, that you may grow thereby."

By being able to admire without the need to acquire, you can save yourself thousands of dollars and years of pain and anguish. You can say to yourself, "I don't have to dust it or clean it. I don't have to insure it. I don't have to paint it, shine it or polish it. I don't have to maintain it. But it sure is beautiful to look at!"

At certain times we feel more envy, like around Christmas time. Or maybe we feel it when we drive through certain neighborhoods or walk through certain malls. There is something that goes on in our minds that says, "You deserve that just as much as the person who has that."

Envy rears its ugly head against anything that might be considered a blessing if that blessing is being received by someone else. And envy has no upside. It's all downhill. All the other sins you can think about start out with some degree of pleasure. Gluttony gives us some pleasure before we gain fifty pounds and have to deal with the ensuing health problems. Anger gives us a pleasing release of pent up emotional energy before we have to deal with the relational fallout and inevitable carnage.

Envy, though, is different. It starts out bad and it stays bad all the way down to the end.

Envy always seeks to level the playing field. It tries either to level us up or to level others down. Envy is defined in one dictionary as an evil eye. And the eye is where the sin begins. We look at what he drives. We see what she is wearing? Our eyes lock onto where they live. And the engines of envy begin to turn.

What happens when we're eaten up with envy? James 3:16 says, "For where envy and self-seeking exist, confusion and every evil thing are there."

When we are envious, when we cannot admire without the need to acquire, we are putting down what God has done in the lives of others. We are ridiculing and rejecting the success of others. We are engaging in gossip and backbiting as we speak ill of them.

As envy eats away at us, it eventually consumes us. Our destructive habit of tearing others down eventually tears us apart.

Psychology Today magazine once conducted a survey of 25,000 people and found that envy is the root cause of a poor self-esteem. People feel inferior only if they compare themselves with someone else and believe that person to be superior. So often, we lose sight of who we are and what we possess because envy reigns in our hearts. And no matter how much talent and money you have, you can always find someone who has more than you.

If we hope to remain in the zone and away from the seduction of the evil eye, we must remain very mindful of two practical areas of our daily life: our reading and viewing habits. Tabloid television programs, gossip columns and so many forms of "entertainment" are rooted in envy. We enjoy reading about the dirty laundry and failures of others. We come away with a smug smile on our faces. "You'd never catch me doing that."

We want to know which movie star has how many homes and which celebrity makes a certain amount of money so we can say, "Why don't I have all of that stuff? That person doesn't deserve that because he or she...." You can fill in the blank with whatever failure or flaw you happen to know about the person.

Proverbs 27:4 reveals that devastating effects of envy and jealousy, "Wrath is cruel and anger a torrent, but who is able to stand before jealousy?"

Envy keeps us from enjoying the success of others, and it keeps us from realizing our own success. It keeps us focused on the ings rather than the Or. And all we can think about is what others have and why we don't have them.

Also, envy denies of the goodness of God. If someone we know closes a huge deal or receives a large inheritance, the evil eye of envy causes us to say, "That should have happened to me instead of to him, because I would have known better how to handle the money."

And when we react like that, we are essentially telling God that he is handing out blessings to the wrong person. But who are we to tell God what to do?

People caught up in envy will also say things like this about the success of others: "Wish I could do that. Wish I could have that. Why does he need that? Why does she have that? So this is what it's like on the other side of the tracks. Someday!"

When you're around people who say things like this about you or other people, head for the hills! They are caught up in the sinister snare of the green eye of envy, and they will drag you out of the zone.

Instead, follow God's bridge of contentment back to the zone and admire the success and blessings of others without the need to acquire them for ourselves. Be prayerful and mindful of how you react when your neighbor buys a new car or you coworker gets the promotion. Be glad for them. Remember that God's blessings are available for everyone, not just you.

Gratitude

There's a second bridge that God has constructed to bring us back to the zone—gratitude. God calls us to develop an attitude of gratitude. An attitude of gratitude not only allows us to be thankful for what we have; it also allows us to rejoice about what others have.

Romans 12:15 reads, "Rejoice with those who rejoice, and weep with those who weep."

The envious person usually reverses this verse. He rejoices with those who weep and weeps with those who rejoice. He becomes so concerned with keeping tabs on everyone around him that he begins to hope others will fail.

Don't be so concerned about what others have to the point that that it causes you forget about being thankful for what you have.

We should weep with those who weep and rejoice with those who rejoice. When we refuse to rejoice with the success of others, we are again advertising our own materialistic mentality. We are attempting to take the focus off our own junk and move the spotlight on to someone else. In short, we are unfairly judging that person.

Are you able to rejoice in the success and prosperity of others? If not, do two things. First, call envy what it is. Quit lying to yourself and to God about the envy you feel in your heart. Admit to God that you have a problem with the green eye of envy.

Second, ask God to develop an attitude of gratitude in your heart. Everyday, thank God for what he has done in your life, and then rejoice in what he has done for others. As you do this, you will break the back of envy and jealousy.

Life in the zone is all about being thankful for what God is doing—not only in our own lives, but also in the lives of others around us.

Generosity

The third bridge back into the zone is generosity. We must learn the secret of generosity. At the very beginning of this book I told you that God is first and foremost generous with us. He is a God of generosity. So in order to pursue God, to live life in the zone, to emulate and imitate God, we need to learn the secret of generosity.

In 2 Corinthians 8:7 Paul says, "But just as you excel in everything—in faith, in speech, in knowledge, in complete earnestness and in your love for us—see that you also excel in this grace of giving."

If we're going to excel in giving, if we're going to imitate the generous nature of our Creator, we must also size up and conquer the enemy of generosity—greed.

I grew up watching professional wrestling. My favorite wrestler was the "American Dream" Dusty Rhodes. And Dusty's signature move was called the Sleeper Hold. He would grab his opponent's neck and head from behind and begin to slowly and forcefully squeeze until his opponent fell to the mat.

A lot of people are caught in the Sleeper Hold of greed. We've allowed greed to sneak up behind us and slowly begin to squeeze our hearts and our minds. And just because you may make a certain amount of money, don't think you are immune. Greed is no respecter of incomes.

The interesting thing about greed is we always seem to notice it in other people, but we rarely see it in ourselves. When you just read the word greed, someone probably came to your mind, but that person probably wasn't you. Sometimes we think of a friend. Sometimes we observe someone from afar. But right now, examine your own heart.

Are you caught in the grip of greed? Or are you practicing the pursuit of God by mirroring his generous character and nature?

If you are not in the zone and you wonder why, maybe

it's because you're hanging around with greedy, selfish people. These negative people are blessing blockers in your life. They are keeping you out of the zone.

1 Corinthians 15:33 warns us against these kind of people. "Do not be misled: 'Bad company corrupts good character.'"

Generous people are upbeat, positive, optimistic and faith filled. I've never met a generous person who was greedy, because generosity is the antidote to greed. I've also never met a generous person who had a negative attitude about life..

At the heart of generosity is the realization that you don't really have something unless you can give it away.

I regularly try to give away something that I like. I'm not talking about giving away old clothes, old shoes or broken toasters. I'm talking about giving away something that means something to you. If you can't give something away, that something has become a god in your life.

That's what greed does. It transforms our goods into gods.

Some of the wealthiest people I've met are bankrupt in the most important areas of life, most especially their relationship with God, because they have not learned the secret of generosity. Their lives are consumed with stuff and the pursuit of more and more and more.

True generosity, however, develops in us when we are free from the preoccupation with things. When things lose their hold on us, when we escape the Sleeper Hold of greed, we are truly free.

GET TO GET VS. GET TO GIVE

If we're going to learn the secret of generosity, we must understand the different motivations for giving and getting. There are two types of getters. The first kind is those people who get to get. Stuff sticks to them like Velcro®. These are the ones who live in the Land of Ing.

Then there are those people who get to give. Stuff just slides off of them life like Teflon®. These are the people who understand that their stuff is not their stuff. They understand the concept of admiring without having to acquire. They know that in order to live in the zone they must be thankful for what God is doing—in their lives and in the lives of others. And they know that to stay in the zone they must overflow with generosity.

While the true motivation for giving should not be to get something back, generosity is always rewarded by God. As we've discovered throughout this book, the rewards are not the motivation behind living in the zone—they are the by-product of obedience. If you give, God is going to bless you—relationally, spiritually, emotionally, financially and in every area of your life. No power on Earth can stop it. To do otherwise, God would have to violate his own nature.

James 1:17 reinforces this spiritual reality. "Every good thing given and every perfect gift is from above, coming down from the Father of lights, with whom there is no variation or shifting shadow."

Satan is building highways of materialism to keep us out of the zone and in the Land of Ing. And when we choose to travel down these highways, we are unable to receive and reflect the blessings of God. But the good news is God has built bridges that circumvent that materialistic mindset and provide a way for us to get back into the zone of God's blessing, back to the tangible and intangible favor of God.

Where are you traveling today? Are you on Satan's highways of guilt and pride? Or are you on God's bridges of contentment, gratitude and generosity?

Let me ask again the question I posed to you at the beginning of this chapter: Where does materialism begin and end? Name the zip code that says someone is materialistic. Name the make and model of car. What size house, which designer labels, what kind of watch, what karat of diamond, what size portfolio, which vacation destination? What income range marks the beginning of materialism?

The answer is, I don't know. And you don't know, either. Humanly speaking, we will never know. Only God knows the answer to that question, because materialism is not defined by a tangible commodity. It's an intangible condition of the heart that is ultimately and only between you and God. And until you go before God and deal with this issue, you will find yourself zoned out and missing out on the real blessings of God in your life. But once you get a handle on the meaning of materialism and you travel on God's bridges, you will stay zoned in to God's sweet spot of success in life.

GET IN THE ZONE
NAVIGATING THE CONSTRUCTION ZONE

- Materialism is not defined by a tangible commodity, but rather by an intangible condition of the heart.

- One of the most dangerous things about money is that if we love it, it will lead us. On the other hand, if we lead it, it will serve us.

- How we use our money can simultaneously diminish the evil one's dominion and make us more like our heavenly Father.

- Doing things God's way, being obedient to God, and being in the zone will result in blessings. Don't let anyone shame you or cause you to second-guess God's hand of blessing in your life.

- When we compare what we've done for God (which is nothing) with what God has done for us (which is everything), our heart naturally overflows with gratitude.

- Once you get a handle on the meaning of materialism, you will stay zoned in to God's sweet spot of success in life.

Matthew 6:24   "No one can serve two masters. Either he will hat the one and love the other, or he will be devoted to the one and despise the other. You cannot serve both God and money."

CHAPTER FOUR

THE CREATURE FROM THE CASH LAGOON

Do you remember the film, "The Creature from the Black Lagoon?" When I was growing up, that movie frightened me more than any other movie I had seen. There was just something in the way it was shot with the black and white film and the coffee black water that got to me. I remember watching those people swimming in the lagoon one minute, only to be dragged into the depths by that hideous looking creature the next. I vividly remember having nightmares about being chased by the Creature from the Black Lagoon.

But I also remember my parents trying to reassure me by telling me that everything was going to be okay. I remember them saying, "Ed, there's no such thing as monsters. They just aren't real."

After studying the material for this book over the past several years, I have to disagree with my parents. There is a real monster. This monster is a big, green, ugly creature that stalks all of us. He's been around for a long, long time. And he can't wait to grab us and pull us under. The monster I'm referring to is called the Creature from the *Cash* Lagoon.

This creature can be just as scary as the Creature from the Black Lagoon was to me as a child. It has the power to grab you and me and drag us out of the zone and into the Land of Ing. It will take us into the murky waters of fear and financial bondage. This monster can ruin your marriage, put your family on precarious financial footing, and leave you floundering in the seas of worry, stress and anxiety.

Maybe you're thinking, "Come on, Ed. There's no such thing as a Creature from the Cash Lagoon. Money is just a means of exchange. There's nothing scary about that."

The reality is, during the past several decades, this creature has moved out of the depths of the lagoon and into the mainstream of life. And this Creature from the Cash Lagoon morphs into several other monsters that can drag us out of the zone.

The Plastic People Eater

The first manifestation of this monster is the Plastic People Eater. Here's how the scenario plays out. We walk down the steep banks of the cash lagoon and we take out our American Express®, MasterCard®, Visa®, or Discover® card. Then we rely on these credit cards to keep us afloat financially. We ignore the signs that say "Warning! Interest infested waters. No swimming!"

We sit back and bask in the sun while we lie on these very poor flotation devices called credit cards and hope that they will keep us alive. And in the sea of life, we may have one floating here and another floating over there. As we drift through life, we think everything is fine. We feel safe and secure because we think we can have the things we want and still float safely on our credit cards. But what we don't realize is that lurking beneath the dark waters is the Creature from the Cash Lagoon.

He can't wait for us to get behind on a few of our payments. He can't wait for our flotation device to get one little crack and begin to leak a little bit. Suddenly, before we realize it, an arm or a leg begins to hang over the side; and the Creature swims up, grabs hold of us and pulls us down—farther and farther into the depths of debt. We can see the surface way up there, and we try frantically to swim. But once the Creature has us in his grips, we find ourselves drowning in debt up to our eyeballs.

Credit cards don't look very scary at first, do they? The Plastic People Eaters aren't intimidating when we have them in our hand. In fact, many of these cards are beautiful and serene. They come in an array of attractive colors and styles. No matter what you're into—football, teddy bears, racing, fishing—you can have it displayed on your very own card.

Credit cards make us feel important. Our name is even engraved on each one in gold or silver. And our wallets are even designed to hold credit cards in a very prominent place.

At first, when we buy something with our credit card, it's absolutely painless. All we do is hand the card to the sales clerk, he or she pushes a few buttons and then we sign. It's that simple.

As we're making these purchases, though, we're out of touch with several sobering facts. We don't think about the fact that 43% of U.S. families spend more money than they make. In fact, according to the Federal Reserve, Americans spend $1.22 for every dollar they earn. We also don't think about the fact that Americans hold a total of over 1 billion credit cards—that averages out to 7.6 cards per household. And the average household carries a credit card debt of over $8400. Here's another staggering statistic: if we make the minimum payment (which is what 65% of cardholders do) on an $8000 balance with an interest rate of 18%, it will take 25 years to pay it off and cost a total of $24,000![1]

The American family is spending more money than it earns. How do we do that? With credit cards! We are buying things with money we don't have. And that unrestrained spending is leading us into crippling amounts of debt to the tune of about $735 billion and rising. Credit card debt is 31% higher than it was just 5 years ago. Personal bankruptcies have doubled in the past decade.[2]

And, sadly, students are watching their parents' spending habits and are getting sucked in by the Plastic People Eaters as well. When the average student graduates college, he or she is likely to have a credit card debt of over $2700. Twenty-five percent of students will owe more than $3000.[3]

The Pulitzer prize-winning columnist Ellen Goodman once said this about the irony of our debt-driven lifestyle: "Normal is getting dressed in clothes that you buy for work, driving through traffic in a car that you are still paying for, in order to get the job that you need so you can pay for the clothes, car, and the house that you leave empty all day in order to afford to live in it."

We've got a serious problem here in the land of the free and the home of the brave. We've become slaves to debt.

The Bible warns of this, "The borrower is a servant to the lender" (Proverbs 22:7).

This text is not saying that you should never borrow money. I've heard people say that the Bible tells us not to borrow money. That's not true. That argument simply will not hold biblical water. Jesus said, "Give to the one who asks you, and do not turn away from the one who wants to borrow from you" (Matthew 5:42).

There are many instances of money being borrowed in the Bible. It is not forbidden. But what we need to understand is that, although we have the freedom to borrow when we need to, we should also have the discipline to only borrow what we can afford to pay back.

Here's the problem: Many of us are on an *American Express* to over spending. And we need to read the *Master's Card* where we will *Discover* a *Visa* to financial freedom.

How do we do that? How do turn our spending habits around and achieve financial freedom? What are our options when it comes to the Plastic People Eaters? How can we keep the creature at bay?

Basically we have two options. The first one is to *use credit cards only for convenience and then pay them off each month*. After all, that is what credit cards were originally designed for: convenience. If we are using credit cards to buy things we know you can't afford, we are being poor stewards of our money.

If you know it is going to be difficult for you to pay your credit cards off each month, then you need to select option number two. *Take out a pair of scissors and cut them up!* And then, don't apply for any more. We get about 50 unsolicited credit card offers every year in the mail.[4] When those offers come, just tear them up.

A good friend of mine is a financial consultant. He had an interesting spin on credit cards that has stuck with me for years. He said, "Ed, you know about the surgeon general's warning on every pack of cigarettes, right? As far as I'm concerned a similar warning should be required on every credit card issued: 'Warning! Overuse can be dangerous to your wealth.'"

That is a good warning for all of us. Credit cards, if not used properly, are a danger to you wealth and your family's future. Don't let the Plastic People Eaters rob you of your financial freedom. Begin today to take the necessary steps to escape the clutches of the credit card monster. If you don't, it will eat you alive.

The Media Monster

Another manifestation of the Creature from the Cash Lagoon is the Media Monster. If you've ever seen Times Square in person or on television, then you can probably picture the mass advertising that is present there. Everywhere you turn in Times Square you see neon lights, ticker tape LCDs, and big screen billboards that broadcast advertisements for every product ranging from shoes to soft drinks, and from clothing to cars. Times Square is the epicenter of commercialism.

What's the drive behind all of these commercials and advertisements? Why do advertisers expend so much time, energy and money coming up with these creative angles and ideas? They do it for one reason, and one reason only—to get us to spend money. Advertising is all about selling you more stuff you don't need. And the Media Monster uses our desire for more, more, more to pull us out of the zone and in the Land of Ing.

How does the Media Monster work? He gets those envy engines really revved up in our lives. He gets us to think, "Oh, if I buy that, then I can be a better person," or, "If I could just have that, then I would be happy."

And what begins as an innocent desire to acquire a few things quickly transforms into living above and beyond our means.

The Media Monster knows that if he can breed discontent in our lives, then he can drag us down. He knows that if he can get us to think that we're not as good as we think we are, we'll jump into the Land of Ing. He knows that if he can mess with our self-esteem, then we're going to take out our wallets and overspend. And once that happens, we are forfeiting our ability to become the kind of people that God wants.

So often we spend out of emotion because we think the ings will give us contentment. And getting new things does have a temporary anesthetizing effect on our problems. There's an emotional high, a buzz that comes from making a purchase.

Then the bills come and reality hits. "I'm drowning in debt!" By the time we realize the Media Monster has dragged us down into the depths of the Cash Lagoon, it's often too late.

So many people right now are messed up because their money is out of whack. They have fallen prey to the Media Monster who tells them that they just *have* to have this or that gadget. And it's a mentality that is easy to buy into—everyone's doing it.

Studies have shown that the average American is bombarded with anywhere from 3,000 to 6,000 commercial advertisements a day. We hear them on the radio, read them in the newspapers and see them on television. The Media Monster is showing its face nearly everywhere we turn. It is beckoning us, enticing us, and pulling us into its lair. It wants to make us think that we can't be happy until we have what it's selling.

But once the shine wears off and the newness fades, we find out it was all an illusion. The commercial hype never delivers what it promises. Advertisements always over promise and under deliver.

Yes, it's okay to have nice things. But recognize the fact that things can never give you the true satisfaction, the true contentment that only Jesus Christ can give. Contrary to the Media Monster, Jesus always delivers on his promises.

Money is great when it's used for the right things. But so often, because of the hype of the Media Monster, we spend too much in the wrong places. And when we overspend we lose the ability to leverage our money for God's kingdom and his purposes.

Before you buy into the Media Monster's promises, recognize that advertising and commercialization are all about selling you things to build up *your* kingdom. And living in the zone isn't about your kingdom. It's about God's kingdom. Jesus' kingdom lasts forever. Ours will pass away. And until we realize that, we will never learn to live in the zone. We need to let our kingdom go and let Jesus reign in every area of our lives, including our finances.

The most practical way to defeat this monster and to stay in the sweet spot of God's success is to learn to say, "No!" Say no to the Media Monster and the thousands of commercial appeals he throws your way everyday.

Have you seen a commercial like this? A ruggedly handsome man is driving a $50,000 decked-out truck down a country road and pulls up to a quaint, beautiful bar that happens to be in the middle of nowhere. He slides out of his manly machine looking like he's walked straight out of *GQ*. As he walks into the bar, a big group of his friends come up to him and give him high fives. Beautiful women come up and kiss him. He's the life of the party. The moment he sidles up to the bar, the bartender has an ice cold glass of beer waiting for him. The announcer says, "It doesn't get any better than this."

Then the commercial ends.

You're lounging in your easy chair at home thinking, "Wow, if I drink that beer, I'm going to look like him and be able to drive a $50,000 custom truck. I'll have a lot of friends and beautiful women will pay attention to me. It'll be incredible!"

But it's all a lie. That commercial can't promise you anything more than a 12-ounce can of fermented hops and barley. That's all it has to offer. In fact, there's an hidden reality conveniently left out of the commercial.

What that beer commercial will not show you is the time this ruggedly handsome guy could not stop at just one cold one. They will not show you the time he knocked down about two 6-packs and blew several hundred dollars buying rounds for his friends. They won't show you that he's up to his blood shot eyes in debt, throwing away his hard-earned cash on booze and struggling to make payments on an automobile he can't afford.

As I strolled through a shopping mall one day, I saw a sign at a jewelry store that read, "Free Gold Bracelets" in giant letters. Underneath it, in small print was this disclaimer: "With a purchase of $250 or more."

I walked a little further to a health food store. There was a giant picture of a popular female celebrity standing beside a workout machine. The unwritten message is, if you use this product, you can look just like a superstar. Most of us, though, could work our entire lives and not look like this celebrity.

Always pay attention to the un-pictured reality. Advertisements are designed to over-promise and under-deliver.

Look at Christ's instructions in Matthew 10:16 (NKJV), "Be wise as serpents and harmless as doves."

Use discernment when the Media Monster comes knocking on your heart. Make sure you ask yourself, "Do I need that? Or do I greed that?"

And recognize the Media Monster for what he really is—another version of the Creature from the Cash Lagoon that is trying to get you to waste you money on things that can never truly satisfy.

The Budget Boogeyman

Another scary monster that the Creature from the Cash Lagoon morphs into is the Budget Boogeyman. And this one can wrap us up so tight that we can't move.

The word budget conjures up a lot of different emotions. Some people look at that word and say, "Budgets are for people who are in financial trouble."

Other people think, "I don't need a budget. I make plenty of money."

Some people are afraid of the word budget because they think, "If I'm on a budget, I won't be able to have any fun."

If you're asking, "Who really needs a budget, anyway?" the answer is, "Everyone."

A budget is basically planned spending. And to understand how to develop a budget, we first need to understand the different types of spending that sabotage the budget process.

Blue Light Spender

Do you remember the blue light specials at K-Mart®? I remember shopping in K-mart as a kid, when all of a sudden the manager of the store would come over the PA system and announce, "We have a blue light special: a blue light special on women's hats."

And every shopping cart would instantly race toward the blue light special at a NASCAR® type pace.

Basically, I'm talking about impulse spending.

As we're casually walking or driving by a store, the Budget Bogeyman has those long arms to reach out and pull us in. He attracts us with sale signs, balloons, and lights. Maybe you've been walking through the mall when all of a sudden you spotted something in the window that you just *had* to have. I know that's happened to me a few times. We may not even need whatever it is. We just have the desire to buy it right then. This kind of emotionally-driven spending is an enemy of planned spending.

Keep-Up, One-Up, Show-Up Spender

The second type of spender is the Keep-Up, One-Up or Show-Up Spender. We buy stuff to soothe our self-esteem. This is what I call ego spending.

In the third chapter we looked at materialism. Materialism drives us to buy things because we think they will make us feel better, make us look better, or give us a shot of confidence.

Think of a married couple in which one of them keeps spending because he or she wants to maintain a certain status, but they can't afford it. So, they just keep racking up credit card debt.

The spouse, though, is afraid to say anything. They don't want to curb the spending or rein in their spouse because they're afraid it will drive them apart or lead to a divorce. That's an example of the Budget Boogeyman rearing its ugly head.

Spending to boost your self-esteem or standing with others will always mess up your budget.

Save It–Blow It All Spender

Finally, you have the Save It–Blow It All spender. This person saves and saves and saves. But then they turn around and spend it all at once. This kind of spender is into the big dollar purchases. The bigger the toy, the better.

Saving money is great. It's an important part of the budgeting process, as we will see. But make sure you know what you are saving for. If you keep raiding your savings to buy big ticket items you don't need, you are jeopardizing your financial future. When your savings is gone and you find yourself in an emergency situation—a job loss or a medical emergency—you will end up having to borrow money just to make ends meet.

The Budget Boogeyman likes it when we turn into these three dysfunctional spenders, because it blows our ability to make and maintain a budget. He knows that the more we spend for all the wrong reasons, the less we'll have to spend for all the right reasons.

Proverbs 27:23-24 says this to help us fight the Budget Boogeyman, "Be sure you know the condition of your flocks, give careful attention to your herds; for riches do not endure forever...."

We have to keep track of our spending. Do you know how much you spent last month? Do you know the condition of your bank account? Or are you just spending away your savings to maintain a lifestyle way beyond your means?

THE B-G-L PRINCIPLE

Let's look at some practical things we can do to escape
the clutches of this dreaded money monster. Because after all,
there are several deadly budgetary blows we can deliver to the
Creature from the Cash Lagoon. And when we follow this plan,
the Creature will fall dead in its tracks and drift back into the
depths where he cannot do any more harm.

To disable and destroy the Creature from the Cash Lagoon,
we need to apply what I call the B-G-L principle. You may be
able to better remember it as the 10-10-80 principle.

Bring

The very first thing that you do to destroy the Creature
from the Cash Lagoon is to bring the tithe back to God. We
covered the tithe in the Chapter Two. Remember, our stuff is
not our stuff. It's God's. And all he asks is that we return ten
percent to him.

Don't fall into the Judas mentality. Judas was taking money
from Christ's ministry box. We would be appalled at stealing
money directly from Jesus. And yet, a lot of us do the same
thing. Malachi 3 tells us that we are robbing God when we
withhold the tithe.

Why should I bring the tithe? Because I'm thankful for
earning money. It demonstrates my understanding that God
owns it all and that I'm just a manager.

Look again at Proverbs 3:9. "Honor the Lord with your
wealth, with the firstfruits of all your crops."

Also, bringing the tithe is accompanied by the promise that

God will supernaturally intervene in our financial affairs. Every time there is a premise there's a promise.

Proverbs 11:24 says, "One man gives freely, yet gains even more; another withholds unduly, but comes to poverty."

I'm not talking about prosperity theology. That line of thinking obligates God to prosper people financially. And that theology is questionable for two reasons. Number one, it limits God and his blessings only to money. And he has many more creative ways to bless us than just with money. Number two, it turns God into a genie, an errand boy; which he is not.

God is sovereign. He is free to bless in whatever way he sees fit. But he promises to bless those who are faithful to him, and he always keeps his promises. As I've said throughout this book, we don't give to get. We get to give. Our motivation for giving is not to receive blessings from God, the Blessor. The blessings are just gracious by-products of being faithful to him.

So the very first step that you must take in order to defeat the Creature from the Cash Lagoon is to bring the tithe into God's house, the local church.

Give

The second step is to give yourself ten percent. Save and invest a minimum of 8-10 percent. And start young.

Look at Proverbs 6:6-8. "Go to the ant, you sluggard; consider its ways and be wise! It has no commander, no overseer or ruler, yet it stores its provisions in summer and gathers its food at harvest."

We are called to mimic the ant. But many of us are failing

at this task, particularly here in America. The average American only saves 4% of his or her income. The average European saves 16%. In Japan, the average worker saves 25%! So to defeat the Creature, we have to get our money working for us.

Once we begin to develop a habit of saving, two things will occur. The first is that we will learn to live on a margin. That means that we will be able to live with less than what we earn. And second, we'll learn contentment. We won't be consumed with envy or greed. Contentment breaks the back of materialism, of the obsession with things.

The world says, "Save for security." The Bible says, "Save for stewardship. Save to show that you're a good manager of God's stuff."

Saving prevents impulse buying, it helps others and it gets your money working for you.

Live

The rest of the money we earn, after you've brought 10% back to God as a minimum worship requirement and saved at least 10%, is left for us to live on. That's the third step in the B-G-L principle. Live on the rest. That means we get to enjoy the rest of our income.

You did not misread that. We get to enjoy the other 80 percent.

I hope you've discovered throughout these pages that it's okay to enjoy the money God's given you. We shouldn't be ashamed of it. And if you're being obedient to him and following a budget, you can enjoy the blessings in your life.

Few people would consider driving a car without a gas gauge. Yet, most people operate without a spending gauge.

Proverbs 13:4 warns us, "Lazy people want much but get little, while the diligent are prospering."

The diligent person, the planner and the strategist all make a profit. It's all about planned spending. We need to dictate terms to our money, not the other way around. We need to tell our money where we want it to go.

Remember, if we lead money, it will serve us. But if we love money, it will lead us. We need to tell it where to go instead of wondering where it went.

So basically, a budget is planned spending. We need to realize that money is an instrument. And we also have to realize that money, not the love of money, is the root of all evil.

God is not opposed to wealth. Abraham, Job, David, Solomon, and Joseph of Arimathea, who were all major players in the Bible, were wealthy men. I mentioned earlier in this book that I met someone years ago who had a foundation with precious stones in it, a driveway with gold, gates that are pearls. You know who I'm talking about. That's God. Is God materialistic? Is God eccentric? No.

God wants us to control our money rather than allowing it to control us. The problem comes when we are weaned on want. And giving into your wants will get you into trouble every time.

THE AVERAGE AMERICAN CHILD

Let me give you a typical example of Al, the average American child. As Al grows up, during the impressionable years of his childhood, most of the conversation he hears around the breakfast table centers on money. His parents are always talking about what money can get, what it can do for them. So Al comes to the conclusion that money really talks.

Then he sees his father climb up the corporate ladder. And because his father is climbing ladder, he gets raises and promotions. Eventually, the family is transferred across the country and they buy a bigger house. Then it happens again, and they get a bigger house. The family is always up-scaling.

As this happens, Al begins to think, "Well, I guess money is more important than spiritual roots or family roots or relational roots. Sounds good to me!"

And Al, the average American child, grows up and considers going to college. He talks to his parents about college and his parents say, "You need to go to that university and major in that subject, because it will yield the highest income. Even though you might not like the field, it is worth it if you make some serious money."

So that's exactly what Al does.

Then he graduates, gets involved in this career, makes a lot of money, gets married and has some children of his own. And Al, having grown up believing that life is all about making more and more money, unknowingly teaches this value system to his children.

Then, as an elderly man, Al looks back over his life, but

he never realizes that he has been led around through life on the short leash by the Creature from the Cash Lagoon. He has spent his life pursuing wealth instead of pursuing God.

This can happen so easily to any one of us. It is real. I see so many of Christ followers being led around by this debt-ridden, materialistic, money-driven mentality. But there is hope. God has a bigger, better plan for us. His plan is not just about making money. It's not about picking the most lucrative career. It's about being true to the person God made you to be. It's about leveraging the gifts, talents and resources he's blessed you with to build his kingdom, not your own. His plan is for you to live in the sweet spot of his success—the only success that, when all is said and done, will ultimately matter.

We've been talking throughout this book about obedience and debt and financial freedom. Spiritually, though, there's a debt we owe that we can never pay. We are all bankrupt. The good news is that God has taken care of our debt by sending Jesus to pay for our sins. The debt has been paid. And to have true freedom, not just financial freedom, we must receive this payment.

If you are ready to discover life in the zone, the very first thing you have to do—before getting your finances in order; before you begin giving; before any of it—is to pursue a vital and vibrant relationship with Jesus Christ. Once you begin that personal relationship with Christ, as you live in obedience to God's life-changing principles of money management, you will find yourself living a life in the blessed place. You will begin to recognize that God is the Blessor. You will begin to realize that you are on the receiving end of the tangible and intangible favor of God. And you will ultimately discover life *in the zone.*

(Endnotes)

1 Sources for the above statistics: CardWeb.com and MyVesta.org
2 msn.com, "How Does Your Debt Compare?" by Kim Khan
3 youngmoney.com
4 startribune.com, "The Higher the Credit Limit, the More Americans Spend," by John Reinan

GET IN THE ZONE
DEFEATING THE CREATURE FROM THE CASH LAGOON

- We should have the discipline to only borrow what we can afford to pay back.

- Use credit cards only for convenience and then pay them off each month,

or

- Take out a pair of scissors and cut them up!

- The Media Monster knows that if he can breed discontent in our lives, then he can drag us down.

- Before you buy into the promises, recognize that advertising and commercialization are all about selling you things to build up your kingdom. And living in the zone isn't about your kingdom. It's about God's kingdom.

- We have to realize that the love of money, not money, is the root of all evil.

- God wants us to control our money rather than allowing it to control us.

- God's plan is for you to live in the sweet spot of success—the only success that, when all is said and done, will ultimately matter.

> ***Matthew 10:16 (NKJV)*** *"Be wise as serpents and harmless as doves."*

ADDITIONAL RESOURCES

Available at CreativePastors.com

God has designed a zone for us where we receive and reflect his blessings. In this study by Ed Young you will learn the keys to living a life In the Zone by dealing with issues of generosity, the tithe, materialism and financial planning.